D0118654

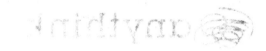

ALTERNATOR
BOOKS™

THE GAY RIGHTS MOVEMENT

ERIC BRAUN

Lerner Publications ◆ Minneapolis

Content Consultant: Finn Enke, Professor of Gender and Women's
Studies, History, LGBTQ Studies, University of Wisconsin, Madison.

Lerner Publications Company
A division of Lerner Publishing Group, Inc.
241 First Avenue North
Minneapolis, MN 55401 USA

For reading levels and more information, look up this title at
www.lernerbooks.com.

Main body text set in Aptifer Slab LT Pro Regular 11.5/18.
Typeface provided by Linotype AG.

Library of Congress Cataloging-in-Publication Data

Names: Braun, Eric, 1971– author.
Title: The gay rights movement / Eric Braun.
Description: Minneapolis : Lerner Publications,
    [2019] | Series: Movements that matter (Alternator Books) | Includes
    bibliographical references and index.
Identifiers: LCCN 2017047416 (print) | LCCN 2017052353 (ebook) |
    ISBN 9781541525573 (eb pdf) | ISBN 9781541523340 (lb : alk. paper)
Subjects: LCSH: Gay rights—United States—History—Juvenile
    literature. | Gay liberation movement—United States—History—
    Juvenile literature.
Classification: LCC HQ76.8.U5 (print) | LCC HQ76.8.U5 B735 2019
    (ebook) | DDC 323.3/2640973—dc23

LC record available at https://lccn.loc.gov/2017047416

Manufactured in the United States of America
1-44407-34666-3/6/2018

CONTENTS

A MOVEMENT BUILDS

In the early morning hours of June 28, 1969, New York City police officers enter the Stonewall Inn, a well-known **gay** bar in the city's Greenwich Village neighborhood. They begin to arrest employees for selling liquor without a license and customers for wearing clothing deemed inappropriate for their gender. But patrons know that the Stonewall Inn is being targeted because most of the employees and customers are gay. The raid is just one in a string of police actions taken

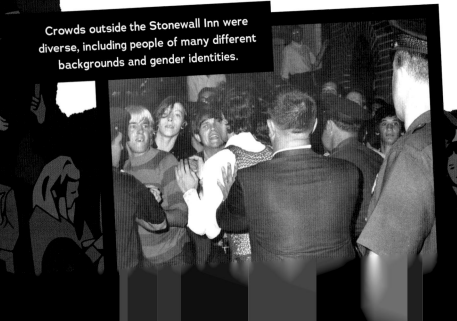

Crowds outside the Stonewall Inn were diverse, including people of many different backgrounds and gender identities.

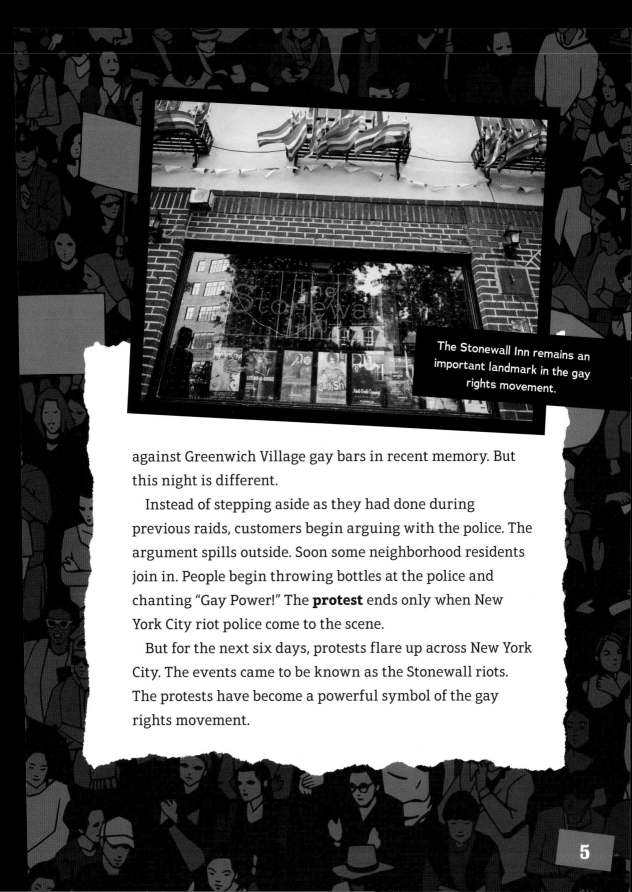

The Stonewall Inn remains an important landmark in the gay rights movement.

against Greenwich Village gay bars in recent memory. But this night is different.

Instead of stepping aside as they had done during previous raids, customers begin arguing with the police. The argument spills outside. Soon some neighborhood residents join in. People begin throwing bottles at the police and chanting "Gay Power!" The **protest** ends only when New York City riot police come to the scene.

But for the next six days, protests flare up across New York City. The events came to be known as the Stonewall riots. The protests have become a powerful symbol of the gay rights movement.

CHAPTER 1

STARTING A MOVEMENT

For much of the twentieth century, most states had laws making gay acts illegal. Gay and lesbian people faced ridicule, hate and, often, physical danger. Many lost jobs or even their homes when employers and landlords learned they were gay. Because of this, most gay people hid their **sexual identity**.

Gay people around the world have been targeted throughout history. In 1895 famous Irish poet, playwright, and novelist Oscar Wilde was arrested for being gay.

As the president of the New York branch of the Mattachine Society, Dick Leitsch staged a legendary "sip-in," in which gay protesters demanded equal service at a bar.

Gay rights groups began to emerge as early as the mid-1920s. But they did not hold public protests or marches, and many of these organizations struggled with keeping members and failed to enact much change.

However, in the 1950s, the more radical rights groups that would lay the foundation for the movement began to form. The Mattachine Society began as a small organization of men who examined their personal experiences of being gay. In sharing their stories with one another, they set out to redefine what it meant to be gay and formed a plan for wider cultural and political change. The organization faced discrimination in new and powerful ways.

Then, in 1955, a group of women in San Francisco formed the Daughters of Bilitis (DOB), one of the nation's first public lesbian rights groups. Two of the founding members were Del Martin and Phyllis Lyon, who later became prominent lesbian rights **activists**. The organization spread, and chapters formed across the United States and Australia. Soon the DOB refocused its attention, becoming a political organization fighting for lesbian rights, a radical move given the discrimination against gay people at the time.

Del Martin (*left*) and Phyllis Lyon (*right*) were among the first gay couples to be married in San Francisco when same-sex marriages temporarily became legal in California in 2008.

Over time, demonstrations for gay rights and gay pride spread across the country. This 1970 march took place in New York.

Following the lead of civil rights and antiwar activists, who held large public **demonstrations**, gay rights activists held demonstrations of their own. In 1965 the first large gay rights demonstrations took place in Washington, DC, and Philadelphia.

GAY RIGHTS GROUPS STEP OUT

The 1969 Stonewall riots continued to strengthen the cause of the gay rights movement. Media coverage of the riots brought wider public attention to those **advocating** for rights. On the one-year anniversary of the Stonewall riots, the first gay pride parades in US history took place in Los Angeles, Chicago, and New York City. And within two years of the Stonewall riots, gay rights groups organized in nearly every major city in the United States. These rights groups represented a diverse group of activists, and while some became more publicly prominent than others, they all made strides toward advancing gay rights.

These men and women take part in the first gay pride march in New York City along Christopher Street.

MARSHA P. JOHNSON was one of the first patrons to protest at the Stonewall riot. She was a well-known figure in the New York City gay community and Greenwich Village neighborhood. Johnson faced many challenges as an African American **transgender** woman in New York City. She spoke out against the injustices at Stonewall and cofounded an organization called STAR with her friend Sylvia Rivera. The group worked with runaway and homeless members of the lesbian, gay, **bisexual**, transgender, and **queer** (LGBTQ) community, especially young people, with an emphasis on helping transgender individuals. Homelessness for youth in the LGBTQ community remains a pressing issue.

Johnson's extraordinary life reappeared in the public spotlight with the 2017 release of a Netflix documentary.

New York mayor John Lindsay was the target of multiple protests. The Gay Activist Alliance wanted Lindsay to take a stand to oppose discrimination against gay people.

Throughout the 1970s, more people joined the cause and activists formed several new gay rights organizations. Some of these groups wanted to take a more active approach to enacting change. The Gay Activist Alliance (GAA) used "zaps" to increase awareness for gay rights. Zaps were public attention-grabbing demonstrations meant to embarrass a public figure who had treated gays or lesbians unfairly, or discriminated against them. One of the earliest targets of zaps was New York mayor John Lindsay, whom the alliance accused of allowing police harassment at gay bars, including the incidents of the famous Stonewall riots.

Meanwhile, many members of the wider LGBTQ community were taking action as well. Many lesbians felt unrepresented by the gay rights movement. Inspired by the success of the 1970s women's movement, they formed their own organizations. Lesbian **feminism** sought to address the issues of sexism and discrimination against lesbians.

A group called the Radicalesbians formed in 1970 to advocate for the rights of lesbian women.

CHAPTER 2

THE AIDS CHALLENGE

In 1981 medical professionals began noticing the first cases of unusual infections and damaged **immune systems** in otherwise healthy young gay men. The mysterious disease spread rapidly. It was later called acquired immunodeficiency syndrome (AIDS). Scientists didn't understand its causes. And there was no cure.

Over the next fifteen years, AIDS spiraled into a full-blown health crisis. By 1995 the disease was the leading cause of death for adults twenty-five to forty-four years old. AIDS killed tens of thousands of people, primarily gay men.

In 1984 Dr. Robert Gallo codiscovered that AIDS is caused by the human immunodeficiency virus (HIV). He pioneered a blood test for the virus and treatment methods for the disease.

FIGHTING AIDS

AIDS had an enormous impact on the direction of the gay rights movement throughout the 1980s. Activists advocated for government funding to study the disease and find a cure. Groups like AIDS Coalition to Unleash Power (ACT UP) staged public events calling attention to the crisis.

ACT UP used public demonstrations called actions to fight for change. The June 1, 1987, action in front of the White House demanded more government funding for AIDS research.

A Moment in the Movement

Larry Kramer was a successful playwright and screenwriter when many of his friends were getting sick and dying from AIDS. Wanting to help, he cofounded Gay Men's Health Crisis (GMHC) to provide social services to people living with AIDS. But soon he wanted to do more to increase public awareness and to bring about political change to fight the AIDS crisis. So in 1987, he founded ACT UP to change both the law and people's perceptions of AIDS, mostly through public demonstrations, or actions. During one action, seven ACT UP members chained themselves to the VIP balcony at the New York Stock Exchange to protest the high price of AIDS drugs. Through these and other widely reported events, Kramer and other ACT UP members helped to change US health policy and raise awareness of AIDS across the country.

Protesters face arrest after speaking out at the New York Stock Exchange against the high price of AIDS drugs.

The AIDS hotline became a valuable resource for individuals with questions about AIDS. The hotline was one place people could go to learn more about azidothymidine (AZT).

Medical science made advances against the deadly disease. In 1987 azidothymidine (AZT) became the first government-approved treatment against AIDS and HIV. Meanwhile, the disease's large impact on communities of color led to more gays of color being represented in the gay rights movement. The landscape of the gay rights movement had changed dramatically in one decade.

CHAPTER 3

MAKING PROGRESS

By the end of the 1990s, fewer people were dying of AIDS. New drugs allowed people with AIDS to live productive lives. Other drugs helped prevent the spread of the virus. Many Americans began to feel less scared of AIDS. But some antigay activists used the AIDS epidemic to criticize LGBTQ people. Even with some social progress, the movement soon faced tough legal discrimination that would shape the next phase of the gay rights movement.

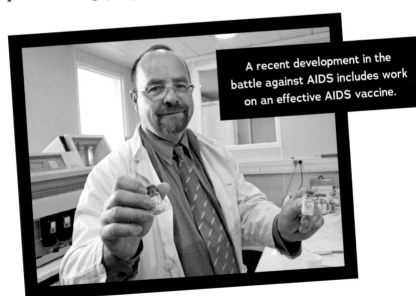

A recent development in the battle against AIDS includes work on an effective AIDS vaccine.

SETBACKS AND BREAKTHROUGHS

One place where the debate over gay rights played out was the military. In 1993 President Bill Clinton signed a policy called Don't Ask, Don't Tell. The policy banned openly gay and lesbian Americans from serving in the military and banned military officers from asking service members about their sexual identity. Gay rights activists criticized the law as discriminatory against gay and lesbian service members. They worked for years to undo the policy. It was finally **repealed** in 2011.

President Barack Obama repealed Don't Ask, Don't Tell, meaning that gay and lesbian service members would be able to be open about their identities.

MARGARETHE (GRETHE) CAMMERMEYER had been in the military for more than twenty-five years. Then, in 1992, the Washington Army National Guard discharged her because she was gay. She filed a lawsuit, claiming discrimination. The judge agreed. Cammermeyer rejoined the National Guard and served as one of the few openly gay or lesbian people in the US military during Don't Ask, Don't Tell. Cammermeyer retired from the National Guard in 1997.

Protesters fighting for marriage equality called for the end to the Defense of Marriage Act as well as state-level laws against same-sex marriage.

In 1996 the community faced a more widespread political roadblock. President Clinton signed the Defense of Marriage Act, which stated that the US government recognized marriage as only between a man and a woman. Soon activists focused on repealing that act too. They began to find success one state at a time. In 2000 Vermont became the first state to allow same-sex civil unions, a legal status that provides many of the same protections as marriage but that is only recognized within that state. Three years later, Massachusetts became the first state to allow same-sex marriages.

A Moment in the Movement

Social acceptance of LGBTQ individuals was a major hurdle for the gay rights movement. In April 1997, the actor and comedian Ellen DeGeneres declared, "Yep, I'm Gay" on the cover of *Time* magazine. As she later told TV interviewer Diane Sawyer, "I decided this was not going to be something that I was going to live the rest of my life being ashamed of." Her statement shocked many Americans. Some attacked DeGeneres for her sexual identity, but many others supported her. Two weeks later, an estimated forty-four million people tuned in to her television show to watch her character come out as gay—a first for a lead character on prime-time television. DeGeneres helped bring public awareness to the LGBTQ community and paved the way for more LGBTQ characters on TV and in movies.

DeGeneres's public coming out included introducing the world to her then partner Anne Heche (*left*).

CHAPTER 4

MOVING FORWARD

Public awareness of many LGBTQ rights issues and especially of transgender rights has grown rapidly in recent years. For example, in 2007 six-year-old transgender girl Jazz Jennings appeared on national television with her family to discuss transgender issues and challenges. Since then Jazz has become a YouTube and cable television star. In 2016 she published a book for teens, *Being Jazz: My Life as a (Transgender) Teen*, and she continues to raise awareness for transgender people.

Jennings is an outspoken advocate. She is one of the founders of TransKids Purple Rainbow Foundation, which supports transgender youths.

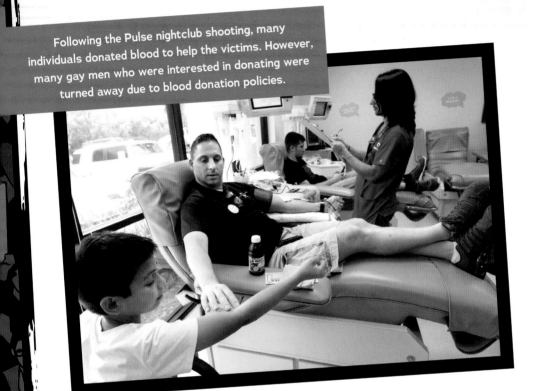

Following the Pulse nightclub shooting, many individuals donated blood to help the victims. However, many gay men who were interested in donating were turned away due to blood donation policies.

Still, the LGBTQ movement has continued to face intolerance and backlash. In an extreme example, in 2016 an antigay terrorist went into Pulse, a gay nightclub in Orlando, Florida, and began shooting. He killed forty-nine people and wounded more than fifty others before the police killed him. Not every example of intolerance is made so public. Many transgender individuals, as well as other members of the LGBTQ community, still face discrimination in jobs, health care, and basic human safety. But as advocates continue to draw attention to these concerns, they continue to bring about change.

THE ONGOING FIGHT FOR TRANSGENDER RIGHTS

Legal successes and challenges for the LGBTQ rights movement have also continued, though. A major victory came in 2015, when the US Supreme Court ruled that state-level bans on same-sex marriage were against the law, making same-sex marriage legal in all fifty states.

Advocates celebrate outside the United States Supreme Court in Washington, DC, after hearing that the court legalized same-sex marriage.

Supporters of the bathroom bill claimed that it protected the safety of women and children. Those opposed, such as the protesters below, said it discriminated against transgender individuals.

Although rights for large groups within the LGBTQ community have expanded, states and the federal government continue to wrestle with transgender rights. One example played out in North Carolina with a 2016 law, officially called House Bill 2 (HB2). Nicknamed the bathroom bill, HB2 made it legal to prevent transgender individuals from using the bathroom of the gender they identify as. Although lawmakers partly repealed HB2 in the spring of 2017, activists have been asking for more, saying the state law still allows for discrimination against gay and transgender people.

Activists are still concerned about legal and social discrimination facing transgender individuals as well as other members of the community. LGBTQ individuals are far more likely to face violence, poverty, and inadequate health-care treatment. Moreover, twenty-eight states still do not protect against gender and sexual orientation discrimination in the workplace, meaning LGBTQ individuals in these states can be fired for the way they identify. While progress has been made, there is still much that needs to be done. The back-and-forth advancement and challenges to LGBTQ rights seem likely to continue as LGBTQ people and their supporters fight for equality.

Learning about LGBTQ history is an important tool in the fight for equality. But there are many different ways of viewing LGBTQ history that are equally important to understanding the past and the LGBTQ rights movement. By pushing to learn more about the diverse voices of LGBTQ individuals, society can begin to work to create a way forward for everybody.

Medical care for LGBTQ youth is lacking in many areas, but some progress is being made. Clinics such as this one in Ybor City, Florida, are being built to meet the needs of underserved individuals, including LGBTQ and homeless youth.

Timeline

1924: The first on-record gay rights group in the United States, the Society for Human Rights, is formed. The group would last less than a year.

1950: The Mattachine Society, one of the first long-standing American gay rights movement organizations, is formed.

1955: The Daughters of Bilitis, the largest national network of activists and consciousness raisers prior to the 1970s, is formed.

1965: Public gay rights demonstrations are held in Washington, DC, and Philadelphia.

1969: The Stonewall riots take place outside the Stonewall Inn in New York City.

1970: The first gay pride parades in US history take place in Los Angeles, Chicago, and New York City.

1972: Parents and Friends of Gays forms to unite lesbians and gays with straight allies. The organization would later change its name to Parents, Families, and Friends of Lesbians and Gays.

1975: The first federal gay rights bill is introduced in the US Congress.

1979: The first National March on Washington for Lesbian and Gay Rights occurs.

1983: AIDS is identified as a rapidly spreading, deadly disease affecting primarily gay men.

1993: President Bill Clinton signs the Don't Ask, Don't Tell military policy.

1995: AIDS has become the leading cause of death for adults twenty-five to forty-four years old.

1996: Clinton signs the Defense of Marriage Act.

1997: Comedian Ellen DeGeneres comes out as lesbian.

2000: Vermont becomes the first state to allow same-sex civil unions.

2003: Massachusetts becomes the first state to allow same-sex marriages.

2011: Don't Ask, Don't Tell is repealed, and gay military personnel can be open about their sexual orientation.

2015: The US Supreme Court rules that state-level bans on same-sex marriages are unconstitutional.

2016: A terrorist kills forty-nine people and injures many others at Pulse nightclub in Orlando, Florida. North Carolina passes the bathroom bill, restricting transgender people's use of public bathrooms.

2017: President Donald Trump announces a ban on transgender people serving in the military.

Source Note

22 Hilary Weaver, "Ellen DeGeneres's Groundbreaking Coming Out: 20 Years Later," *Vanity Fair,* April 28, 2017, https://www.vanityfair.com/style/2017/04/20th-anniversary-of-ellen-degeneres-coming-out.

Glossary

activists: people who work to bring about social or political change

advocating: working to support a cause

bisexual: a person who is romantically attracted to people of their same gender or to those of another gender

demonstrations: public gatherings protesting against something or expressing views on a political issue

feminism: a movement advocating for women's rights

gay: a person who is romantically attracted to a person of the same gender. A lesbian is a gay woman.

immune systems: networks of cells, tissues, and organs that work together to defend against disease and other threats

protest: an organized public demonstration expressing strong objection to policies or laws. Protesters are individuals who attend a protest.

queer: an individual who is romantically attracted to a person of the same gender or who identifies as a person who does not fall into the gender categories of man or woman

repealed: revoked or canceled

sexual identity: how one thinks of oneself in terms of whom one is romantically attracted to

transgender: a person whose gender identity or expression differs from what is typically associated with the sex he or she was assigned at birth

Further Information

Braun, Eric. *Taking Action for Civil and Political Rights*. Minneapolis: Lerner Publications, 2017.

Heitkamp, Kristina Lyn. *Gay-Straight Alliances: Networking with Other Teens and Allies*. New York: Rosen, 2018.

Kids 4 LGBT Rights Now
https://kids4lgbtrightsnow.wordpress.com

Kingston, Anna. *Respecting the Contributions of LGBT Americans*. New York: PowerKids, 2013.

One Million: Kids for Equality
https://onemillionkids.org

Pohlen, Jerome. *Gay & Lesbian History for Kids: The Century-Long Struggle for LGBT Rights, with 21 Activities*. Chicago: Chicago Review, 2016.

Stevenson, Robin. *Pride: Celebrating Diversity & Community*. Custer, WA: Orca, 2017.

TransKids Purple Rainbow Foundation
http://www.transkidspurplerainbow.org

Index

Photo Acknowledgments

The images in this book are used with the permission of: New York Daily News Archive/Getty Images, p. 4; Glynnis Jones/Shutterstock.com, p. 5; Library of Congress (LC-DIG-ppmsca-07756), p. 6; New York Post Archives/Getty Images, p. 7; AFP/Getty Images, p. 8; © Jesse-Steve Rose/The Image Works, p. 9; © Ellen Shumsky/The Image Works, p. 10; Tibrina Hobson/Getty Images Entertainment, p. 11; Santi Visalli/Archive Photos/Getty Images, p. 12; © Ellen Shumsky/The Image Works, p. 13; Bettmann/Getty Images, p. 14; Bettmann/Getty Images, p. 15; New York Daily News Archive/Getty Images, p. 16; Mario Ruiz/The LIFE Images Collection/Getty Images, p. 17; ANNE-CHRISTINE POUJOULAT/AFP/Getty Images, p. 18; JEWEL SAMAD/AFP/Getty Images, p. 19; Kim Komenich/The LIFE Images Collection/Getty Images, p. 20; Bill Clark/CQ-Roll Call Grou/Getty Images, p. 21; Peter Jordan/PA Images/Getty Images, p. 22; Featureflash Photo Agency/Shutterstock.com, p. 23; Orlando Sentinel/Tribune News Service/Getty Images, p. 24; Alex Wong/Getty Images News, p. 25; Boston Globe/Getty Images, p. 26; ZUMA Press Inc/Alamy Stock Photo, p. 27. Design: Stephen Rees/Shutterstock.com (torn edges border); Amitofo/Shutterstock.com (crowds); Milan M/Shutterstock.com (grunge frame); Miloje/Shutterstock.com (texture background); rob zs/Shutterstock.com (protests); Kair/Shutterstock.com (raised fist title treatment).

Front cover: Library of Congress (LC-DIG-ppmsca-09729) (top); s_bukley/Shutterstock.com (right); John Arehart/Shutterstock.com (bottom); Stuart Monk/Shutterstock.com (left).